the
emotional
buddy
system

In the sea of depression
your buddy is your lifeline

Eugene James Baston

The Emotional Buddy System
In the ocean of depression, your buddy is your lifeline.

First published in Australia by Eugene James Baston 2025
www.theemotionalbuddysystem.com

A catalogue record for this
book is available from the
National Library of Australia

ISBN: 978-1-7641702-0-8 (pbk)
ISBN: 978-1-7641702-1-5 (ebk)

Typesetting and design by Publicious Book Publishing
Published in collaboration with Publicious Book Publishing
www.publicious.com.au

Dedication

To those who've known the darkness—
this book is for you.

And to those who stood beside them through it all—
the supporters, the silent warriors,
the ones who never let go.

"A friend loves at all times, and a brother
is born for adversity."
— Proverbs 17:17

Your presence is powerful.
Your love is a lifeline.
You are not alone.

Table of Contents

Letter from the Author

Dear Reader,

Many years ago, I was snorkeling alone on a reef in the islands of Fiji. I had been chasing a school of fish across the coral when, suddenly, I found myself in deep, open water. Panic set in. I was disoriented, far from the reef, and completely alone. I frantically swam to the surface and eventually made it back to the beach—exhausted, shaken, but safe.

I remember thinking: *I will never dive alone again.*

The ocean is a beautiful place—but it can also be dangerous when you're alone.

It would be years later that I'd learn about the scuba diving buddy system—the life-saving practice of never diving solo. But long before I heard of that system, I had already experienced something similar on land: the emotional buddy system.

Let me explain.

For as long as I can remember, I've had bouts of depression. My earliest memory of it was as a teenager. Though it didn't last long, the intensity was overwhelming—deep sadness, hopelessness, and tears I couldn't explain. Back in 1981, when I first experienced that shift in my inner world, there was no one to talk to. No one who understood.

I remember going to my parents. Their response was:

"Snap out of it—or else."

I asked, "Or else what?"

"Or else we'll send you away somewhere."

That was over 40 years ago. So what's changed?

How have I not only survived but, in many ways, flourished—while living with what I call the volcano within?

The answer, without hesitation: buddies.

At different points in my life—especially the most critical ones—there have been people who showed up. Some were like passing ships in the night, offering brief but vital encouragement. Others have stayed by my side for years. Each one has mattered. Each one has played a life-saving role in my life.

Opening up about how I felt wasn't easy—especially as a male Australian, where the culture tends to stigmatize expressing one's inner feelings.

But I have learned that silence isolates and that healing requires honesty and openness. I once spoke about my depression in front of 3000 people in a stadium in Central Europe. Sure, it took courage to speak up on the subject, but through this amazing experience, the healing benefits were not only personal. Many approached me after and, for the first time, talked openly about their own struggles with depression.

I've experienced both roles: the one *in* depression and the one *walking with* someone through it.

I know how damaging words like *"Snap out of it"* can be. And I also know how powerful it is when someone simply says, *"I'm here for you. Tell me how it feels?"*

Even my mother, who loved me dearly, struggled to understand. In my thirties, she would say, *"Can't you see the blue sky beyond the clouds?"* Or *"There must be a reason you're feeling this way."* She meant well. She just didn't understand that depression doesn't need a reason. No one *wants* to feel this way. No one volunteers for depression.

So, what genuinely helps?

There are many helpful tools—medication, exercise, sleep, nutrition, and therapy. But without a buddy—whether a parent, a friend, a partner, or a doctor—you're essentially diving alone in the dangerous ocean of depression.

I remember the reef in Fiji. And I remember being 14, alone in my bedroom, consumed by a sadness I didn't understand. Neither place was safe. Neither place was survivable without support.

Fast forward to 1995. I was 28. A kind older woman invited me for tea after hearing I was struggling. Her first words surprised me:

"Eugene, I've never had a depressed day in my life."

In that moment, I wondered, How can she possibly help?

But then she gently offered me something I'll never forget. She handed me a notebook and pen and said, *"Why don't you write down what you're feeling? Then I'll take you to the doctor myself. If you can't speak, I'll speak on your behalf."*

And she did. She kept her word.

She showed me that a buddy doesn't need to have experienced depression to be a lifeline. They just need to Care.

Years later, I learned about the scuba buddy system. And eventually, I made the connection: Emotional support is a kind of diving buddy system. It saves lives—not by fixing anything, but by staying present, watching for signs, and surfacing together.

So please, read this short book with an open mind and heart. Whether you're struggling yourself or walking with someone who is, I hope it helps you see the power of *not going it alone.*

Because there is a buddy out there for you.

You don't need to dive alone.

On a Final and Very Serious Note:

My experience with depression has ranged from passing moments of sadness to overwhelming, suicidal thoughts. While sadness can often lift with time, **suicidal thoughts must always be taken seriously**.

In 2018, while living in Central Europe, I faced one of the darkest moments of my life. It was early morning, and without warning, the **volcano within me erupted**. Within minutes, I was overtaken by a powerful, consuming urge to end my life. I was alone—and at work.

I walked to my car, opened the door, and sat behind the wheel. As I stared ahead, preparing for what might have been my last act, something unexpected happened: a flood of memories came rushing in. I thought of all the people who had stood by me over the years—especially my dear wife and son. I remembered the truths I had shared with others when I had been *their* buddy during dark times.

Those memories became anchors for my soul. They didn't fix the pain, but they slowed the spiral. They reminded me that I had choices.

In that moment, three options came to mind:

1. Call emergency services
2. Drive to the hospital
3. Go straight to my doctor

I chose my doctor—and within minutes, I was sitting in his office. The care I received that day was nothing short of **life-saving**.

Please hear this clearly:

Depression's voice cannot be trusted. It is not your compass. It is not your guide. When it tells you there is no hope, it is lying.

Over the years, I've been blessed with buddies who didn't suffer from depression themselves—but who had a balanced, grounded perspective. Their loving, steady presence helped readjust my thoughts when I couldn't see clearly. That kind of mental and emotional *recalibration* can be a literal lifesaver.

But when the weight becomes too much—**don't carry it alone. Reach out.** Call your doctor. Go to the hospital. Dial 000 if you are in Australia or your country's emergency line wherever you are. You matter too much to disappear.

As you turn the final pages of this book, I hope its message becomes more than words—I hope it becomes a **lifeline**. May *The Emotional Buddy System* offer you the clarity, the courage, and the connection you need to keep going.

Because no one should dive alone.

With all my heart,

Eugene James Baston

Introduction

There are moments in life when words fail. When someone you love disappears into themselves, when silence replaces laughter, and when the spark you once saw in their eyes fades into a quiet that unsettles the soul. These are the moments that call for something deeper than advice.

They call for presence.
They call for gentleness.
They call for a kind of love that stays close, even in the darkness.

I've seen what depression can do.
I've felt its weight in my own life,
And I've watched it wrap itself around people I care about, making it hard for them to speak, to function, even to breathe at times. And yet, in those deepest, hardest moments, one thing has always made the difference: **connection**, friendship, a buddy by your side.

This book was born out of that understanding.

The Emotional Buddy System is not a textbook.

It is not clinical or complicated.

It is human. Simple. Profound.
It offers a framework rooted in something beautifully ordinary—how divers survive beneath the sea.

What makes diving safe is the buddy system.

No diver descends alone. No one surfaces alone. And if one runs out of air, the other shares theirs—without hesitation.
Isn't that exactly what we need in our emotional lives?
In these pages, you will find more than insights—you will find **a new language for support**, one that helps you:

- Show up without fixing
- Stay close without intruding
- Offer hope without pressure
- And rise together, even when the ascent is slow

Whether you are the one in pain or the one offering your hand, this book will speak to you. It will comfort you. And perhaps, most importantly, it will remind you that **you are not alone**—and were never meant to be.

Read it with your heart open.

Let its truths settle into your relationships.

And remember: even in the depths, there is breath. There is light. There is a way forward.

Together, we surface.

No One Dives Alone.

Some journeys are too deep to make alone.

Ask any diver. Before they enter the ocean's depths, they are trained in one foundational truth: **never dive alone**. Beneath the surface, in a world without words, danger can appear without warning. Panic can strike. Air can run out. And in that moment, the difference between survival and tragedy is often this—**having a buddy**.

A partner.

A presence.

Someone within reach who knows the signals, shares their air, and rises with you.

This is more than diving advice.

This is a model for surviving depression.

When Depression Pulls Us Under

Depression is like deep water.

It's dark. It's disorienting. It slows everything down.

Sometimes, it makes it hard to breathe—to hope, to speak, to even want to surface.

And too often, people try to survive it alone.

They hide their pain. They withdraw. They lose their voice underwater.

But what if we had an emotional equivalent of the dive buddy?

What if no one had to face the depths of depression in silence?

The Emotional Buddy System

This book was born from a single idea:

What keeps us alive underwater can also keep us alive in the emotional world.

Using the principles of the diving buddy system, this book offers a new way of approaching depression, whether you are:

- The one **struggling**, searching for hope, or gasping for emotional air
- The one **standing beside** someone in pain, unsure of how to help without making it worse

Each chapter parallels a key principle of diving with a deeply human truth about mental health:

- How to check in meaningfully before the descent
- How to stay within reach when words fall away
- How to share your breath—your hope—when someone runs out
- How to learn and respond to silent signals
- How to rise slowly, together, without leaving anyone behind

A Book for the Struggler and the Supporter

This book isn't a clinical manual.
It's not filled with diagnoses, stats, or prescriptions.
It's a **companion guide**—gentle, real, and hopeful.
It's for the person who doesn't know how to explain what they're feeling.

It's for the friend, partner, or parent who wants to help but is afraid to say the wrong thing.

It's for anyone who believes that **presence matters more than perfection**—and that **love can breathe life where silence once suffocated**.

You Don't Have to Have All the Answers

You just need to stay close.

To ask. To notice. To share your air when someone's running out.

To believe that even slow healing is still healing.

And that surfacing—even from the deepest pain—is possible when you do it together.

This book is your guide.

To walk with someone through the dark.

To ask for help when you're underwater.

To become fluent in the signals of the heart.

Because no one should have to face the depths of depression alone.

Let's dive in—together.

Chapter 1

The Pre-Dive Check — Emotional Check-Ins That Save Lives

Diver's Log

Every diver knows: before you enter the deep, you stop and check your gear.

You don't rush. You pause. You run through the essentials—**oxygen, regulators, buoyancy, weights**—because once you're submerged, fixing a missed problem could be too late.

This is called the **pre-dive check**. It's simple. It's routine. And it saves lives.

So why don't we do this in life?

When someone we love is sinking under the weight of depression, anxiety, or inner turmoil, we often don't know what to say. We tiptoe, avoid, or assume they'll tell us if something's wrong. But depression doesn't work like that. It hides. It isolates. It whispers, "Don't burden anyone."

That's why we need to borrow from the diving world— and bring the pre-dive check into our relationships.

You Don't Have to Be a Therapist. You Just Need to Show Up.

In scuba diving, your buddy doesn't need to be an expert technician. They just need to be present and attentive. The same is true emotionally.

Your role isn't to diagnose, fix, or lecture.

Your role is to notice, ask, and listen.

Here are the kinds of simple, powerful "emotional pre-dive checks" that matter:

- **"How are you today, really?"**
- **"What's been heavy on your heart lately?"**
- **"Is there something you've been holding in that you'd like to get out?"**

They're small questions. But to someone silently battling despair, they're oxygen. They're care. They're permission to start breathing again.

Why These Check-Ins Matter

People who are struggling often won't reach out—not because they don't want help, but because they can't. The effort it takes to ask can feel impossible. So they wait. And they hope that someone will notice.

When you offer a check-in, you break through the isolation. You say:
"I see you."
"You matter."

"You don't have to carry this alone."

Like a diver checking their buddy's gear before descent, you could be the one who prevents a deeper crisis just by asking a question.

Practice Makes Presence

Don't wait for someone to look like they're falling apart. Make emotional check-ins part of your normal rhythm with people you care about, especially those who have battled mental health challenges before.

Send a message. Leave a voice note. Ask the deeper question. And if you're the one struggling, know this: You're allowed to ask for a pre-dive check, too.

Final Thought: Catch It Early. Stay Close.

Emotional health, like deep-sea diving, can be dangerous if ignored.

The deeper we go into ourselves, the more important it is to have someone on the surface, watching, caring, ready to pull us back if needed.

The emotional pre-dive check is one of the most powerful tools we have.

It's not fancy. It's not complicated. But it could save a life.

And that life might be your own, or that of someone you love.

Chapter 2

Stay Within Reach — The Power of Consistent Presence

Diver's Log

In diving, a buddy never swims too far ahead or lingers too far behind. They stay close—**within sight, within swimming distance**—so that if something goes wrong, help is immediate. Not delayed. Not distant. Immediate.

This rule of proximity is not just for physical safety. It's for emotional security. When you're in the deep, knowing someone is close calms the panic, steadies your breath, and reminds you: *you are not alone.*

The same is true when someone is navigating the dark waters of depression.

Emotional Proximity Doesn't Require Constant Contact

You don't have to talk every hour or even every day. You don't need to fix anyone or have all the right words. **Your presence just needs to be felt.**

- A text that says: *"I'm thinking of you."*
- A voice note: *"No need to reply. Just wanted you to hear a friendly voice."*
- A short visit or even a shared silence on the phone.

To someone battling inner storms, these small gestures are **anchors**. They may not pull someone out of depression, but they remind them there's still a line to the surface—and someone's holding on.

You Matter. I'm Here.

People in pain often feel invisible. Depression isolates. It whispers lies like:

- "No one would notice if you disappeared."
- "You're a burden to everyone."
- "You're too much." Or "You're not enough."

Staying within reach cuts through those lies. You don't have to make grand gestures. Often, the smallest ones are the most powerful:

- Sitting beside someone in silence.
- Dropping off their favorite snack.
- Sending an old photo with the caption: *"Remember this day?"*

Each act says: *You matter. I'm here.* And sometimes, that message is what keeps a person breathing.

Stay Steady, Stay Gentle

Just like in diving, you don't swim up and down too quickly. You **match your pace** with your buddy's. If they're having a low day, you don't try to rush them out of it. You simply remain close.

It takes patience. Presence. And a quiet kind of love that says:
"I'll walk this with you. No matter how slow. No matter how long."

Final Thought: Your Nearness Is Their Lifeline

When people say, *"I don't know what to say,"* they often do nothing.

But silence can be filled—with presence, care, and gentle reminders that love doesn't vanish in the dark.

So stay close. Stay reachable. You don't have to be perfect. You just have to show up.

Because healing doesn't always happen in breakthroughs.

Sometimes, it happens through **being within reach**— day after day.

Chapter 3

Share Your Air — Share Hope

Diver's Log

Every diver is trained to carry a second air source, often called an *octopus*. It's not for themselves—it's for their buddy. If something goes wrong underwater, if a regulator fails or air runs low, this backup can save a life.

They share air.

It's a simple idea with a life-altering impact. And it's just as essential in the emotional world.

Because in depression, people can run out of emotional "air" too.

When Hope Runs Out

Depression drains more than energy.

It empties joy. Purpose. Breath.

The sufferer may look fine on the outside, but inside, they're gasping—struggling for reasons to get out of bed, to speak, to live.

When that happens, what they need most is not someone to *fix* them, or lecture them, or push them to "snap out of it."

What they need . . . is someone to share their air.

What It Means to Share Your Air

You may not be able to give them answers. But you can offer what you *do* have:

- **Share your calm.**
  Sit with them in silence. Be the presence that helps them breathe again when their mind is spinning.
- **Share your memories.**
  Tell stories of better times. Remind them of who they are beyond the darkness—what they've overcome, the laughs you've shared, the quiet triumphs they may have forgotten.
- **Share your belief in them.**
  Speak gently but truthfully: "*I believe in you, even when you don't.*"
  That sentence alone can be a breath of life when someone feels like they're drowning in doubt.

Hope Is Contagious

Just like oxygen, **hope can be transferred**. Not forced. Not faked. But passed gently—breath by breath—from one soul to another.

Sometimes, the person suffering doesn't need to *do* anything right away. They just need to know that someone sees them, stays with them, and refuses to give up on them.

When you lend your hope, you're saying:
"*You don't have to believe in a better day right now. I'll believe for you until you can again.*"

That kind of love can save lives.

Final Thought: One Breath Can Make All the Difference

In diving, when someone runs out of air, it's not a lecture that saves them. It's **air. Shared. Immediately. Without hesitation.**

In life, it's the same.

If someone around you is gasping emotionally, offer your breath.
Your calm. Your care. Your memory. Your faith.
You might be offering the one thing they didn't know they needed to keep going.

Sometimes, the most powerful words are the simplest:
"**I've got you.**"
"**You can borrow my air until you find yours again.**"

Chapter 4

Know the Signals — Learning to Read What Isn't Said

Diver's Log

In the deep ocean, divers don't speak. There are no words. No conversations. Instead, they rely on **hand signals**—clear, simple gestures that communicate vital information. A fist to the chest means "*I'm out of air.*" A thumbs-up means "*Let's surface.*" A flat hand waving side to side? "*Something's wrong.*"

These signals aren't just helpful. They're life-saving. If a diver misses the signs, the consequences to their buddy can be fatal.

The same principle applies in the emotional depths of depression.

Depression Has Its Own Signals

When someone is suffering, they may not tell you. In fact, **they often won't**. Not because they don't want support, but because pain makes it hard to speak. Fear, shame, or numbness may silence the words.

So instead of saying, "I'm not okay," they cancel plans. They stop replying to messages. They withdraw. Their tone becomes short, or they say they're "just tired." Sometimes, they disappear into their bed or their screen, hoping someone will notice but fearing they'll be seen.

These are the emotional hand signals.

And your job—if you want to be an emotional dive buddy—is to learn them.

Not to pressure. Not to pry. But to *notice, acknowledge,* and *respond with care.*

Responding to the Silent Signals

You don't have to guess exactly what's wrong. You just have to show you've noticed—and that you care without judgment.

Try:

- "Hey, I noticed you've been a bit quiet lately. Just wanted to check in."
- "You don't have to talk, but I'm here if and when you want to."
- "Want to go for a walk? We don't even have to talk—we can just be."

These gentle responses let the other person know:

"I see you. I'm not here to fix you. I'm here to walk with you."

And that makes all the difference.

Sensitivity Saves Lives

When a diver misses a signal, it can be fatal. When a person in emotional distress feels unseen, unheard, or misunderstood, it can reinforce the belief that *no one cares*.

But when someone notices—when someone says, "*You matter, and I'm paying attention,*"—it interrupts that dangerous narrative.

It plants a seed:

"*Maybe I'm not invisible. Maybe I'm not alone.*"

Sensitivity doesn't mean you absorb someone else's pain. It means you stay open. Observant. Compassionate.

You listen not just to words but to silence, to changes in energy, behavior, and tone.
You become fluent in the unspoken language of emotional survival.

Final Thought: Learn the Language of the Heart

Not everyone will say, "I need help."
But almost everyone will *show* it—if you know what to look for.

So pay attention.
Not with judgment. But with gentleness.

Learn the signals. Respond with care.

Be the one who notices the silence—and stays close until the words return.

Because just like underwater, in the depths of depression, **noticing a signal can save a life**.

Chapter 5

Surface Together — The Grace of Slow Healing

Diver's Log

In diving, no one surfaces alone.

As the dive ends, buddies begin their **ascent together**, side by side, rising slowly. Too fast—and the body suffers. Too slow—and the buddy may be lost in the deep.

So they move as one.
Pacing each other. Watching. Waiting. Supporting.
It's not just protocol—it's protection.

The same is true in emotional healing.

Healing Is Not a Sprint

Recovery from depression is not fast.

It is not linear.

There is no magic moment when the clouds suddenly part and the sun stays out forever.

Healing is a **slow ascent**—a gradual resurfacing after being underwater for too long.

Some days, it feels like progress. Other days, it feels like slipping backward. But if you're moving—even inch by inch—you're still rising.

And when you're rising together with someone, the journey feels a little less heavy.

Walk (or Float) Beside Them

An emotional dive buddy doesn't rush the person they're supporting.

They don't say:

- *"You should be better by now."*
- *"Just think positive."*
- *"Hurry up and move on."*

Instead, they match their pace.
They adjust.
They stay present during the pauses, the regressions, and the setbacks.

They say:

- *"Take your time. I'm not going anywhere."*
- *"Whatever pace you need, I'll walk it with you."*
- *"Even if we surface one breath at a time, we'll get there."*

Even Slow Progress Is Progress

In a culture obsessed with instant results, it's easy to feel broken if you're not getting "better" fast enough. But healing doesn't respond to pressure—it responds to presence.

Every small step counts:
- Getting out of bed
- Sending one message
- Saying "yes" to one small thing

Celebrate the little victories.
And when your friend or loved one can't celebrate, celebrate for them.
Remind them that **movement is enough**, even if it's barely visible.

Final Thought: Together, You Rise

Just like in diving, the ascent is safest—and strongest—when it's shared.

No one needs to be left behind.
No one should feel rushed.
And no one should have to find the surface alone.

So rise slowly. Steadily. Side by side.

And remember this truth:
Even when the journey feels endless—when done together—it becomes survivable.
And eventually . . . beautiful.

Together, you rise.

Conclusion

You Were Never Meant to Dive Alone

We have journeyed through the depths together—learning how to **check our gear** with honest conversations, **stay within reach** through simple acts of presence, **share our air** by offering calm and hope, **read the silent signals** of distress, and finally **surface side by side** in a slow, patient ascent.

What the Buddy System Really Teaches Us

1. **Connection Is Survival**
   Isolation is the true enemy in depression. Every chapter has shown that the smallest thread of connection can be the strongest lifeline.

2. **Presence Beats Perfection**
   You don't need the perfect words or expert skills. Showing up—consistently, gently, humbly—is what changes outcomes.

3. **Hope Is Both Fragile and Transferable**
   Like a second regulator underwater, hope can be passed from one person to another. Shared hope multiplies; hoarded hope withers.

4. **Healing Has Its Own Pace**
Progress is rarely dramatic. It's measured in breaths, not leaps. Respect the tempo of recovery—yours or someone else's.

Your Next Steps

1. **Choose Your Dive Buddy (or Buddies)**
Identify one or two people you trust enough to ask, *"Will you check in on me and let me check in on you?"* Make it explicit; clarity empowers.

2. **Schedule Regular Pre-Dive Checks**
A weekly text, a standing coffee date, or a simple "How are you—*really*?" ritual can keep small struggles from becoming silent crises.

3. **Create an "Air-Sharing" Plan**
Decide together what you'll do if one of you starts to run out of emotional air—maybe a code word, a shared playlist, or a promise to call before things spiral.

4. **Learn and Teach the Signals**
Share how you each manifest stress or sadness. The better you understand one another's non-verbal cues, the faster you can respond with compassion.

5. **Commit to Surfacing Together**
Whether it takes weeks or years, agree that neither of you will rush the process—or leave the other behind. Slow, steady progress counts.

A Final Word

To the One in the Depths . . . and the One on the Surface

To the One in the Depths of Depression

If you're reading this while still underwater, please know this:

You are not broken.
You are not weak.
You are not invisible.

I know the weight you're carrying. It presses on your chest like the ocean itself, and some days, even the act of breathing feels like too much. Hope may seem faint, like a light far above—but it is not gone. It flickers in small things: a kind word, a quiet presence, a steady hand.

Somewhere out there—maybe closer than you think—**someone is willing to share their air with you**. They can't fix you, and they don't need to. All they need to do is be beside you while you float, while you drift, while you find your way back.

Please let them.

Even if you're not ready to speak. Even if your breath is shallow.

Take it in—just one inhale of borrowed strength, one borrowed heartbeat of hope. That's how it begins.

You don't have to surface today. But you don't have to stay at the bottom alone, either.

You are not a burden. You are worth the rescue.

To the One on the Surface

If you're the buddy holding the line, know this:

You don't need the perfect words.

You don't need to fix the pain.

You just need to *stay close*.

Your presence is the medicine. Your willingness to show up again and again—even in silence, even in uncertainty—is what makes the difference between drowning and surviving.

There will be days when your person pulls away. There will be times when you will say, *"I don't know what to do."* That's okay. You're not a lifeguard. You're not a savior.

You're a buddy. And that is more than enough.

Keep offering your steadiness. Keep showing up without demands.

Keep the light on. Keep the signal clear:

"You're not alone. I'm here. I'll rise with you."

That's the miracle. Not fixing, not forcing—just staying.

And if your own lungs feel tired from helping someone breathe, don't forget: *You're allowed to come up for air, too.* Being a buddy means caring for yourself as well.

The surface is wide enough for both of you.

www.ingramcontent.com/pod-product-compliance
Lightning Source LLC
Chambersburg PA
CBHW051211090426
42740CB00022B/3470